# THE SEED OF MY WOMB

## PAULETTE M. VANDERHORST

Palmetto Publishing Group
Charleston, SC

The Seed of My Womb
Copyright © 2019 by Paulette M. Vanderhorst

First Edition

Printed in the United States

ISBN-13: 978-1-64111-410-3
ISBN-10: 1-64111-410-X

# MONDAY, FEBRUARY 11, 2002

Coming home from work and visiting my father-in-law who is in the hospital. Drove across the railroad tracks and Lo Mann friend came running to my car. I said, "Why are you running?" He said, "Mrs. Paulette, I sorry, I shoot Lo Mann. We was playing with the gun." I said, "All I want to know is my son dead?" He said, "No, ma'am," so I jumped out of the car, ran in the house, and saw my boy lying between the door of his room and the den. The instant I saw my boy lying there I said, "Oh Lord Jesus, please help us," then I kneeled down to my boy and said, "Okay, you have to pray for yourself. You can't go off my prayers. You have to call on God for yourself." Immediately, my boy started praying, and I said, "Oh, that's the way." He was dying, and I said to my brother Robert, "You have to keep talking to him. Don't stop," as I tried to keep Kesia, Jasmine, and DeShawn together. As Daddy and Jenly try to help me, my son's friend had already called the EMS, and they were on the way. Although I didn't know where the gunshot wound was, I did know that God was in control, and always will be. I was saying, "Lord Jesus, I know I am always bothering you. Please, I need you even more, please, Jesus." I rode in the EMS truck and was thanking God my son was still alive, and saying, "No weapon formed against you shall prosper." The ride in the EMS truck was not long, but the people seemed like they didn't want to move out of the way. When we arrived at the hospital, that's when it came down on me heavy, because I was not sure where the gunshot wound was. I could not see him for a long time. The doctors talked to me, explaining that as soon as they found out, they would come and get me. It took a little while. I had so much support from both sides of the family; church members, coworkers, everybody. Thank you, God, for loving and caring people. The doctors came and got me to see him about two hours later. When I saw him, I kissed him as I cried, saying, "Thank you, Jesus." God is good all the time, and all the time, God is good. I thank God for everyone who was there for me, because I sure did needed it. I spent the night and my sister-in-law Denise stayed with me. Words cannot express how I feel. Overwhelming. He has tubes everywhere; nose, mouth, chest. To keep him alive, breathing machine, IV, etc. I got up all through the night to check on him.

# TUESDAY, FEBRUARY 12

All the doctors came around and explained to me what happened, where the bullet is, and what's to be expected. According to the doctor, the bullet went through the left side of his neck, then straight through his cervical at level C5, leaving him paralyzed from the neck down. In my heart and mind, I am saying, "That's not what God say," but I was thanking the doctors because I appreciate all that they are doing for my son. He rest pretty well. Members of lovely Mountain, Roper Hospital staff members, family, friends, and members from Mount Moriah were very supportive. I thank God for everyone.

# WEDNESDAY, FEBRUARY 13

T he doctors came in talk to me about his condition again. He said a .32 caliber left him in critical condition, paralyzed, but God is our healer, and we know he is in control. I was exercising him two or three times a day. He had so much visitors until I finally had to slow it down a little in a good way, because he couldn't talk, and he was getting frustrated and blood pressure was going up. Had a pretty good day considering what happened in his life. God is good. Thank you, God, for saving Wendell Manigault's life. He got a little angry because no one could read his lips. When they called me to see if I could understand him, he said he wanted to die. I said to him, "Wait a minute, if you were supposed to die, you would have just as soon as you got shot. God save you for a reason. I don't want to hear talk like that again." I prayed for him. We rebuke the devil, and know that God is our healer. We had a good day the rest of the day.

# THURSDAY, FEBRUARY 14

Valentine's Day. He is coping better with what has happened, still in good spirits. The nurses and doctors are very good with Wendell, explaining everything that they do. They are helpful in every way. The nurses are very loving, caring, god-like people. We had lots of visitors everyday; special, overwhelming. They are trying to get him off the breathing machine. He is not able, so have to do surgery on Monday, February 18.

# FRIDAY, FEBRUARY 15

A nother blessed day. We are coming along. Every day it gets better. He's a little more alert. He is trying to use his lips a little more. Ready to eat one day at a time. I left for a while to see your daddy (Wendell Sr.). Daddy (Robert Tindal Sr.) came and surprised us.

# SATURDAY, FEBRUARY 16

Your grandfather (Robert Manigault) died. You had a good day, lots of visitors; people from all over. Your daddy spent the night Friday and Saturday.

# SUNDAY, FEBRUARY 17

---

G ood day, lots of visitors, but I didn't let too much visit you, because
you needed to get your rest for Monday.

# MONDAY, FEBRUARY 18

Went into surgery for tracheostomy, then the doctors came to speak with me and Wendell; however, I was already prayed up since 5:30 a.m. He went to surgery at 9 a.m., then he came out at 10:30 a.m. The doctors came to me and said, "Everything is good." Thank you, Lord. I know God is in control.

# TUESDAY, FEBRUARY 19

Another nice day. OT and PT came to do therapy with Wendell. I have been exercising him everyday. You are still coming along just fine. Your dad, Jasmine, and Kesia came by. We all stayed with you. We didn't go to the wake for your grandfather (Robert Manigault).

# WEDNESDAY, FEBRUARY 20

I got up to exercise Wendell, made sure he had his bath, then my friend Jametta Hamilton came and sat with him for me until I got back from the funeral. Before I left, Wendell said he felt the bullet in his neck, but he was feeling the tracheostomy, so we got him a mirror to show him what was in his throat. He had a little moment. He didn't look mad, but it was touching. We will get through this. We can do all things through Christ that strengthens us.

# THURSDAY, FEBRUARY 21

He had a very busy morning working on his breathing. He just had a rough day, so we just let him relax for the rest of the evening. He ate strawberry ice cream, did good.

# FRIDAY, FEBRUARY 22

Wendell had a very good day. His morning started off good. The doctors are talking about how good he is doing. He sat up in the wheelchair today for about twenty minutes; that was good. I have already started my job bathing him, feeding, catheterizing, suctioning, etc. He is doing good with his breathing.

# SATURDAY, FEBRUARY 23

I woke up about 8:30 a.m., went and got something to eat for breakfast. Went and got Wendell ready to start the day. I got him bathed and turned, and all that good stuff. We just chilled out and watched movies most of the day. He started having visitors, some young ladies and men from school, and family members. Corey came in and he would not leave out when he come in. He is Lo Mann's bodyguard. He drunk seven glasses of water, but still do not have much of an appetite. Just Jell-O and juice. I know it will get better. God, I thank you for this day. Everyday it gets better; more improvement each day.

# SUNDAY, FEBRUARY 24

I thank God for one more day. I got up, checked on Lo Mann, but he was still asleep. So I came back out and got some breakfast, me and Tina Mack. Went back in to check on Lo Mann and talk for a little while. Leatrice came by, sat in with him for a while. Kenneth came by, sat in with him for a while. Jametta came in, sat with him for a while. Leatrice and I went to the store, got him two shirts, and me a couple of outfits, and some personal things for the both of us. I came back to the hospital and took a shower, then Denise and I went to wash him up and put a shirt on him. He had a good day. Breathing on the vent mostly by himself, he is doing good. Thank God.

# MONDAY, FEBRUARY 25

One day at a time. Got washed up. He got a little upset because he doesn't like to be turned from side to side, but it is good for him not to get bed sores or pneumonia, so he is angry right now, but he will be all right. It is a part of PT. They downsized his tracheostomy from an eight to a six. He sat up in his wheelchair for forty minutes. He did really good. He is a very strong man, trying to do the best he can. We are going to make it with Jesus.

# TUESDAY, FEBRUARY 26

G ood day. I got Wendell bathed before 9:30 a.m., catheterized etc. He sat up for thirty minutes in his wheelchair. No vent, breathing on his own he had a good day. Kind of quiet not saying much.

# WEDNESDAY, FEBRUARY 27

Joy Kinsley from Roper, one of my coworkers, came over and spent the night, and I went home. That was very special and nice of her. Words cannot measure how I feel. Thank God for people who are loving and caring. I love everybody, and everyone has been praying, caring, sitting, good spirits, helpful in many ways, loving, thoughtful, smiles, tears of joy, calling, cards, money, food, etc. Thank God for treating people the way you want to be treated. It pays off in the long run.

# THURSDAY, FEBRUARY 28

Joy Kinsley still there with Wendell. I had a little running around to do. He sat up for one hour and forty-five minutes, thank God. Moving out of ICU to room 714. God is good all the time. Kesia and Star came to relieve Joy. She went home about two-ish. That was special. When I came, he was already in his room set up. He had a pretty good night. I talked to him a little bit about faith and will power. I know he can do it. God is in control. We pray together every night.

# FRIDAY, MARCH 1

Pretty good starting morning. Got up, try to get him to eat. Not working. I gave him a bath. The nurse came in and did her thing. The PT/OT came in and got him up sat up for an hour. Pastor Dayson came in and had prayer. Sister Shirley Ravenel came in. We had a good day. Four boys from school, Auntie Denise, and Alice, Granny Liz, Jasmine, and Wendell, two girls from school. He's always having visitors; school, church, my coworkers, family members on both sides. Lots of love. Ronald and two girls came to visit. I took Jazz to Granny's house about 10 p.m. Came back to hospital, did my routine, and went to bed. We had another blessed day.

# SATURDAY, MARCH 2

We decided to lay back and relax until ten-ish. We did. I got up, bathed, and catheterized him, then we put on clothes. Two of his friends came by and I took a shower as they visited with him for a long while, encouraging him to eat. Pretty good day. It's raining nasty outside. We just talked, watched TV, then he got a little upset because of his breathing, and I told him it's going to be all right. He said he want to kill that nigga, then I told him, "No, let's not think like that. I know it is easy for me to say, but in the process of your healing, let's go through it not with hate but love, because God is going to work this out, believe it. Let's continue to love the young man no matter what, and let's lean on Jesus to bring us out, and he will." We just talked about what happened, but he did not tell me the same story the boy told me. Lo Mann said it didn't happen like that; he said he wasn't playing with his gun. Lord, please, it is in your hands. No weapon formed against us shall prosper. Daily routine. I fell asleep about 11 p.m. I was still up reading the Bible and just having a little talk with Jesus and thanking him for Wendell's health and healing, and Reverend Robinson gave him a verse to remember, Psalms 30:2: "Oh Lord, thy God, I cried unto thee, and thou has healed me." Thank God for all the ministers and deacons and missionaries from all over. It is a blessing. I am not worried because my

*Paulette M. Vanderhorst*

God is an on-time God. I just thank God for peace and understanding, love, joy, and being able to stand, for he is the reason. Can't nobody do us like Jesus. He is our everything. We love you, Jesus. Thank you for another blessing.

# SUNDAY, MARCH 3

We got up, bathed, dressed, and listened to church on TV. He had a good day. We had visitors after church. Deacon Dan Ravenel came by and gave me communion first Sunday. Wendell Sr., Jazz, and I kind of sat around, laughed, and played games. We had a good day. Wendell Sr. is getting used to what we will have to do in terms of taking care of our son.

# MONDAY, MARCH 4

G ot up, bathed and dressed. The respiratory nurse came, OT and
PT came. He got up for two hours, went downstairs. Auntie Nette
came by and helped us sit up. We had a good day.

# TUESDAY, MARCH 5

We got up, bathed and dressed. Wendell Sr. and I was getting Wendell Jr. ready for his trip to Roper Rehabilitation Hospital. Wendell Sr. spent the night. He must have gotten up every time he heard noise. Everything went well. I was packing things. Wanda Reese was helping me and Wendell Sr. carry the luggage to the car. We sure have a lot of things, I guess, for twenty days in the hospital. Everyone was nice, loving, caring, helping, and we appreciate everything they have done for us. Word of encouragement from all over. The hospital we left about 1:45 p.m. came in room 885, met lots of specialists, coworkers, doctors, and friends. God's gift from heaven.

# WEDNESDAY, MARCH 6

We woke up on the eighth floor at Roper Hospital. I got up, took a shower. Alice Burst, OT, came in, got Wendell bathed and dressed, and gave him a complete check over to see what is what. Mark, the PT, came in, and we sat him up in the chair. He got dizzy for a minute or two. While in the chair he only can sit up at a forty-five-degree angle for right now. He sat up for two hours. That was good. Linda Collins, the social worker, came in. Dr. Elizabeth Rittenberg and Dr. Warmoth came in talk to him and examined him. Everyone is so special, caring, and loving. They are a blessing from God. Kim, the recreational therapist, came in and talked to him. Speech person Elizabeth came in and talked to him. The ENT doctor came in and downsized his tracheostomy from six to a four. God is good all the time. He is talking just a little. Called Granny, Jazz, and Kesia, and told them hi, and Robert Jr., Aunt Denise, and school teacher Miss Windham came by. Lots of my coworkers. Everyone is so caring. Thank you, God, for special people.

# THURSDAY, MARCH 7

P astor Dayson came by with a word of encouragemen. Strong believer, and special prayer. Thank God for my pastor. I got up, bathed, and dressed. Wendell is still sleeping, waiting on OT to come and help him bathe and get dressed. Mary Lou is his primary nurse. He got the best nurse. Reverend Robinson came by with a word of encouragement and prayer. Talk to Wendell. Jesus is the key, and he remembered the verse he gave him to remember. Sat up for two hours. My boss over the rehab unit came in and prayed for Wendell. It was about twenty of us, going good. She sent up a wonderful prayer for my son. It is a blessing. Thank you, God, for special people. We had a meeting. He will stay at Roper Rehab for five or six weeks. They will do everything, and all that they can do. Also, whatever we need at home. Thank you, God, for your blessing.

# FRIDAY, MARCH 8

---

Went to check on some business. Wendell Sr. and I came to Mann's swallowing test. Everything went really good. He passed the test. He will be able to eat mechanical, soft and thin liquid, small sips and bites. He is talking a little. Thank you, God. He sat up for two hours. He has been doing a wonderful job. God is good all the time. Thank you, God, for all your blessings each and every day. Can't nobody do us like Jesus.

# SUNDAY, MARCH 9

I called to check on Wendell. He is fine and in good spirits. Thank you, God. We got down to the hospital about 1:30 p.m. Wendell Sr. got him up in the chair for an hour with the assistance of my coworker Mark. He did a good job. Sister Ancrum came by. Reverend Bratton and his wife came by. Wendell Sr., Jr., and myself watched two movies together. I enjoyed that. We laughed and talked. We had a good day. Ordered pizza; he just ate three bites. I called Pastor Dayson. I wanted him to hear Lo Mann talk on the phone. He said he made his day. I called Pastor Robinson. He was just as excited, too. He talked to Wendell. God is good. He said to be patient, and wait on God. I love my pastors.